RELIGIOUS SCHOOLS: THE (

Introduction

(1) Religion and Schools: the historical background

(2) Philosophical Arguments Against: an overview

(3) The Autonomy Argument: some further considerations

(4) Church Schools: educators or indoctrinators?

(5) In defence of religious schools?

(6) Conclusions and Policy Recommendations

Introduction

Churches on Sundays may be standing emptier than ever, but church schools on weekdays are frequently having to turn away students, such is their popularity. Religious schools are being widely heralded as a great success story. The recent government green paper *Building on Success* (March 2001) says:

> Schools supported by the churches and other major faith groups are, of course, valued by members of those groups. They also have a good record of delivering a high quality of education to their pupils and many parents welcome the clear ethos of these schools. We therefore wish to welcome more schools provided by the churches and other major faith groups and by other voluntary and community groups, where there is clear local demand from parents and the community.

Many see this as unobjectionable. Indeed, some would see it as a human right. The 1998 *Human Rights Act* goes so far as to say:

> In the exercise of any functions which it assumes in relation to education, and to teaching, the State shall respect the right of parents to ensure such education and teaching in conformity with their own religious and philosophical convictions.

Practical as well as principled reasons are offered in support of religious schools. Many cite evidence that students in religious schools perform better than in non-religious ones. One consequence of this is the common spectacle of non-religious parents pretending they have a deep commitment to a school's religion in an attempt to make sure their children get into a 'better' school.

However, religious schools, particularly state-funded ones, raise important moral and political questions for everyone. This is because of the general importance of education, the ways in which religious groups can use it as a means of increasing their power and influence, and perennial anxieties about the relationship between church and state. These arguments are not getting much of a hearing, as the consensus builds for expanding the number of religious schools.

This pamphlet is an attempt to put those serious issues back onto the agenda. We do not believe that the proposed expansion of religious schools sector is justified. Further, our reasons for believing this have repercussions for the way in which such schools are regulated and for the teaching of religion in all schools. We argue (perhaps against the tide of popular opinion) that schools need to be less religious. This is not at root an anti-religious argument. Indeed, we believe that the principles we argue for and on which our policy recommendations are based should appeal to the religious and non-religious alike. The idea that creating more religious schools is a benign, just and socially desirable project is deeply flawed, and it is time those flaws were clearly exposed. That is what this pamphlet aims to do.

(1) Religion and Schools: the historical background

Relations between schools, religious groups and states have taken many different forms. Theocracies like Calvin's Geneva, Imperial Russia or contemporary Iran, have insisted that all educational institutions teach the truth of a single official religion. At an opposite extreme, 20th century secular dictatorships, like Stalin's Russia, have banned religious teaching, along with religious worship, in any form. Here, however, we restrict ourselves to exploring the way more or less liberal states, which allow their citizens to practise the religion of their choice, have regulated church-school relations.

Ever since the 18th century, liberalism has been inseparably associated with principles of religious toleration and with the separation of church and state. Early liberal thinkers like Montaigne, Locke, Spinoza, and Voltaire argued against the view that it was the job of the state to force its subjects to adhere to one religion rather than another. Many Enlightenment thinkers, moreover, criticised traditional, confessional educational practices on the grounds that they were sectarian, superstitious and impractical. Perhaps it is surprising then, that very few nations, even self-avowedly secular-liberal ones, have instituted a rigorous separation of church and school.

The one obvious exception is provided by the US. As is well known, the First Amendment of the American constitution stipulates the separation of church and state: 'Congress shall make no law respecting an establishment of religion, or prohibiting the free exercise thereof'. This reflected both the ideals of Enlightenment deists like Jefferson and Madison, and the recognition by more traditional Protestants that, unable as they were to establish their own sect in power, religious freedom was preferable to the establishment of someone else's sect. It was not until the Civil War however, that the First Amendment began to be interpreted as applying to state as well as federal government – before then most states promoted one Christian denomination or another – and it was even longer before it was applied to schools. True, during the course of the 19th century, many states

established publicly funded 'common schools', the ancestors of today's
public school system, but although these were neutral between different
Protestant groups, they were emphatically Protestant. Teaching was based
on 'the Bible, the spelling book and the primer'. It was only in the last
quarter of the 19th century, and largely as a grudging concession to Catholics
and Jews, that public schools began to take on a genuinely secular character,
and even then only in the big Eastern and Midwestern cities. Indeed, the
most significant steps towards a genuine prohibition of state-funded
religious schooling were not taken until the 1960s, when the Supreme Court
issued a series of opinions banning school prayer or bible reading in public
schools. These decisions, moreover, have proved extremely unpopular with
the religious right, which has campaigned to reverse them ever since. In the
1980s President Reagan unsuccessfully proposed a constitutional
amendment protecting prayer in school, while more recently President Bush
has expressed his support not only for prayer in school, but also for a
voucher system that would permit state-funding of confessional religious
schools. Many Christians also want to see 'creationism' taught alongside
evolution in biology classes, with surveys suggesting that less than a half of
American adults believe that humans evolved from earlier species.[1]

In contrast to the US, most European nations now pursue a more pluralist
approach. This is true even of France, a nation that, like the U.S., has a
strong secular republican tradition dating back to the 18th century. The
French Revolution nationalised or seriously curtailed the confessional
activity of France's Catholic schools. The Restoration re-established
Catholicism as France's official religion, and Catholic schools have
received some degree of public funding ever since, though the Third
Republic (1871-1940) established a rigorous separation of church and state
that survives to this day. The present constitution stipulates that France is a
secular republic, which will favour no one religious view over any other.
As a result there is a strict prohibition of any form of religious expression
in France's public schools. Though religion can be studied from a
comparative perspective, religious education as it is understood in this

---

[1] See James W Frazer, *Between Church and State; Religions and Public Education in a Multi-Cultural America*, Macmillan, Basingstoke, 1999.

country (the sympathetic exploration of - mainly Christian - religious beliefs and practices) is proscribed, and the wearing of the Islamic headscarf by female students has been a matter of controversy. At the same time, however, private religious schools that have been in existence for at least five years are entitled to state financial support in exchange for agreeing to follow certain curricular guidelines. This policy is unpopular with many secular republicans and teaching unions, especially as French governments have been reluctant to support Islamic schools on the same basis as Christian ones. For the time being, however, it remains a feature of the political landscape.

The situation in the rest of Europe, including England, is similar in many respects to that in France (although the UK is almost unique in Europe in retaining an established church). English schools were the creation of the Church. It was for instance, voluntary church societies (the non-conformist British and Foreign School Society and the Anglican National Society) that first developed a national system of elementary schools in the first third of the 19th century. By the 1860s, however, it had become clear to most that voluntary church societies could not alone meet the educational needs of the nation. Hence, the Elementary Education Act of 1870. In debates leading up to the act, radicals, inspired by Jeremy Bentham, argued for a wholly secular educational system, while many clergymen wanted an expansion of church schools. The Act went for a compromise. Voluntary schools were allowed to continue with the help of grants-in-aid, but they were to be supplemented by state schools run by local school boards. These local schools were prohibited from promoting one denomination over another, and parents were given the right to withdraw their children from religious instruction. At the same time, schools were obliged to offer Christian instruction of a non-partisan kind.

This arrangement has remained more or less unchanged to this day. The 1944 Education Act, for instance, while revolutionising the educational system by extending the school leaving age to fifteen and providing for a new generation of secondary schools, continued to provide for religious schools. These were now offered the option of increased state funding and control as 'Voluntary Controlled Schools' or lesser state support and greater independence as 'Voluntary Aided Schools'. Under the act, the provision of school worship and religious instruction became obligatory in all state schools. Indeed RI was the only subject that the act required all state schools to teach. Despite the dramatic decline in church attendance and Christian belief in the intervening period, the 1988 Education Reform Act extended and reinforced the old arrangements, which had largely fallen into disuse. Thus, religious worship 'wholly or mainly of a broadly Christian character' is now compulsory, and while religious education now has to take account of all 'the principal religions' practised in the country, it also has to reflect the fact that 'the religious traditions of the United Kingdom are in the main Christian'. There is no requirement to study Humanism, atheism or agnosticism as alternatives to religious belief. The RE syllabuses of voluntary aided schools (as distinct from the more heavily funded voluntary controlled schools) are not controlled by public government bodies at all, but are set by Church of England or Roman Catholic authorities.

Today, just under a third of all English publicly funded schools have a religious foundation, catering for 23% of all school pupils: 12% at Anglican schools, 10% at Roman Catholic ones. Church schools have the enthusiastic support of the present Labour government. Thus, the recent Green Paper on education, *Schools: Building on Success* (February 2001), welcomes the Church of England's desire to open a hundred new schools and promises to encourage an increase in the number of state-funded religious schools generally, especially schools catering for Muslim, Sikh, Greek Orthodox and other minorities. To this end, it is planned to reduce the financial contribution required from the church or faith 'from 15 per cent to 10 per cent for capital items, and to remove the contribution altogether for revenue items'.

In England at least, we are a very long way from a rigorous separation of church and school.

(2) Philosophical Arguments Against: an overview

In the light of this historical background we will now set out what we see as the case against religious schools. It should be noted that some of the arguments (if successful) tell against the <u>existence</u> of religious schools, while others count only against the <u>state funding</u> of such schools. The first set of arguments to be considered will be objections <u>in principle</u> to religious schools and/or to state support for them. Objections in principle will first be presented in outline, together with the possible replies to them. We will identify the most telling line of argument, and then develop this in greater depth. More practical arguments will be considered later: about the place of religious schools in contemporary society and, in particular, the question of whether they are likely to lead to an increase or decrease in sectarianism and racism.

Before dealing with the arguments, though, we need to define 'religious school'. By 'religious school' we mean a school which intentionally encourages its pupils to have particular religious beliefs and which regards such encouragement as a significant part of its mission. Religious schools often have other important characteristics, such as admissions policies that favour churchgoing parents, or partial funding by religious bodies, but the <u>defining</u> feature of religious schools (and the one which gives humanists most cause for concern) is that they attempt to instil particular religious beliefs in their pupils. On our definition, church schools may or may not be religious, though in practice almost all of them will be. Conversely, a school could be religious without being owned or run by a religious organisation.

(a) 'Religious Belief is Undesirable'

The first argument against religious schools is simply that because religious belief is undesirable, and religious schools encourage religious belief, religious schools are undesirable (because they encourage something undesirable).

The main problem with this argument is the status of the claim that religious belief is undesirable. Certainly many people, including many humanists, think that all religious beliefs are false, irrational, or harmful. This may or may not be true. But it is undoubtedly a highly <u>controversial</u> claim, even within humanism, since not all humanists are <u>anti</u>-religious (as opposed to merely <u>non-religious</u>). Hence, the argument is weak insofar as it relies on a strongly anti-religious premise. It would be better to produce an argument based on more widely accepted assumptions (and indeed this is what we will be doing later).

(b) Evidence

The second argument claims that schools should teach only knowledge and evidence-based belief. Therefore, since there is no firm evidence for (e.g.) the existence of God, belief in God's existence etc. should not be taught.

This argument suffers from similar problems to the first, though perhaps to a lesser extent. For the claim that there is no evidence for the existence of God (although endorsed by many humanists) is highly controversial and has been the subject of philosophical and theological debate for centuries.

Also problematic is the idea that schools should teach only knowledge and evidence-based belief. Surely, it could be argued, this requirement is too tough. After all, where would it leave subjects like drama, literature, music, and sports?

Finally, setting our standard of evidence at the right level could prove difficult. If it is set high, so that only things about which we're fairly certain are taught, then education may become extremely cautious (and boring!) and even some well established scientific theories (such as the 'big bang' or evolution) could be ruled out. But, if the standard of evidence is set low, then religious beliefs might be taught alongside (say) relatively speculative historical or scientific theories.

(c) State Neutrality

A third argument says that the state should remain neutral with respect to religion and certainly should not promote (for example, by funding) one religion over another.

The main problem with this argument is that, even if the principle of state neutrality is accepted, it does not <u>obviously</u> follow that there should be no state-funded religious schools. For there may be several different ways of being neutral. One is not to fund religious schools. But another is to fund various different kinds of religious and non-religious school and to offer parents a choice.

So while this argument does tell powerfully against a system in which one religion is privileged (such as present position in England) it does not necessarily count against a more pluralistic system of state-funded religious schools. We will return to this issue shortly.

(d) Children, Autonomy, and Consent

The fourth and final argument, which we regard as the strongest, is rather different from the others in that it focuses on children's autonomy, or rather their lack of it. The fundamental premise of the argument is that, given the importance of fundamental religious and value commitments to a person's life, such commitments should be entered into only subject to all the normal requirements for valid consent: in particular, competence, full information, and voluntariness. Religious schools, however, are likely to violate these requirements – partly because of (younger) children's lack of autonomy and partly because of the nature of such schools' missions.

Taking each element in turn, <u>competence</u> to assess religious views can plausibly be said to be lacking in children, or at least younger children, because of their lack of experience and incomplete cognitive development. This fact, it is claimed, means that we should not expose children to religious instruction, because to do so would be to take advantage of their vulnerability and to induce in them a belief system to which they are not in a position validly to consent.

Full information is likely to be lacking in religious schools because the information that they impart will be biased towards a particular religion. What is required for full information is an unbiased account of all the options available, including humanist and other non-religious options.

Finally, children's adoption of the school's preferred religion may not be truly voluntary, depending on what teaching methods are used. In some cases, children are reprimanded for not accepting (or not appearing to accept) the religion in question, in which case their acceptance is involuntary because it is coerced. More commonly, subtler methods of undermining the voluntariness of the child's decisions are deployed - such as a general assumption of belief, confusion of moral values with religious ones, compulsory worship and prayers.

A major advantage of this line of argument is that it looks as if it can avoid getting entangled in substantive debate about the truth or otherwise of religious beliefs, since it is grounded not in the claim that religious beliefs are false but rather in a principle of autonomy – which would hold even if (say) conventional Christianity were true. Indeed, the autonomy argument could even be used against certain kinds of humanist school (if such things existed), because the argument's target is not so much the content of what is taught, but rather the way in which religion is likely to be taught in religious schools. Religious education, teaching children about different religions, is acceptable according to the autonomy argument. What is not acceptable is religious instruction or indoctrination which can lead to the non-autonomous acquisition and holding of significant beliefs. (We will return shortly to the task of defining more precisely the difference between 'religious education', 'religious instruction', and 'religious indoctrination'.)

The autonomy argument against religious schools is, then, the strongest. Its two main attractions are: (a) that it appeals to a principle (the principle of autonomy) to which many people, religious and otherwise, would subscribe, and (b) that it does not rely on other substantive arguments about the truth/falsity or desirability/undesirability of religious belief itself.

(3) The Autonomy Argument: some further considerations

Having briefly set out the autonomy objection to religious schools, this section will now look at some of the replies to it which the defenders of religious schools might offer. We will begin with some rather simplistic replies which can be fairly easily dealt with, and then move to a more serious reply. In dealing with this the nature of the autonomy objection will be more fully elaborated. This will lead us back to our three earlier objections, and we will see that more nuanced versions of these do have some force and fall into place in the context of the elaborated autonomy objection.

Someone who sincerely believes in God might reply to the autonomy argument as follows. First, given the truth and importance of belief in God, children must be made (as far as possible) to believe in God, even if this means that they do not come to believe in God by means of an autonomous decision. Crudely put, getting them to believe in God is more important than ensuring that their religious beliefs are autonomously acquired. Second (the believer may argue) given that the religion in question is true and that the alternatives - including Humanism - are false, the earlier point about full information doesn't hold. For when children are taught religion they are given full information: i.e. the truth.

There are, however, good counter-objections to these points. First, autonomous commitment to beliefs is something which religious believers ought to value, as many do. For religious belief or any other kind of value commitment is surely worthless unless it is something with which the person has genuinely identified and which is wholeheartedly theirs. Compare, for example, a 'genuine' conversion to Christianity resulting from bible study and contemplation with a belief in Christianity caused solely by brainwashing and mind-affecting drugs. Surely the belief in the first case is worth more because the person has <u>given</u> herself to Christ, whereas in the latter case the person hasn't given herself at all but has rather <u>been taken</u>. Similarly, the religious commitment of someone who is simply unaware of any alternative is surely of less value than that of someone who has chosen that belief over other alternatives because they find it compelling. The latter person's commitment is of more value because it results from a positive act of <u>self-determination</u>.

As regards the full information point, however committed someone may be to the truth of a religion, they cannot reasonably assert that teaching one religion, or even possibly several religions, only from the perspective of that particular religion provides full information. If there are other sets of beliefs, religious and non-religious, to which many other people are sincerely and deeply committed, then children have not been given full and unbiased information on which to make up their own minds unless they have been taught impartially about those alternative beliefs and why people hold them. Nor will they have been fully educated about the society in which they live and the range of beliefs found in it.

We turn now to a more serious reply to our argument, one which starts from an acceptance of what we have said about the value of autonomy. Defenders of religious schools may object that we are assuming a caricature of what such schools are actually like. They do not, it may be said, set out to indoctrinate or manipulate their pupils. They do not drill them into a mechanical acceptance of religious beliefs. They respect their pupils' autonomy, and though they may welcome religious commitment, they wish it to be freely chosen, in the light of a full knowledge and understanding of alternative views.

It is true that there are many conscientious teachers of religious education, both in religious and in non-religious schools, who take their role as educators very seriously and who aim to teach their pupils about the full range of theistic and atheistic beliefs in an open-minded, critical and rational way. Having acknowledged that, we nevertheless maintain that there are certain distinctive features of religious schools which, by their very nature, run counter to those sincere aims. We have defined a 'religious school' as one which 'intentionally encourages its pupils to have particular religious beliefs and which regards such encouragement as a significant part of its mission.' We have distinguished church schools from religious schools and have acknowledged that the former may not necessarily be the latter. We argue, however, that in practice church schools typically are religious schools (in the defined sense) and that this inevitably compromises whatever commitment they may profess to the value of autonomy.

The concept of autonomy makes two distinct contributions to that argument. First, as we have seen already, the fact that children (or at least younger children) lack autonomy should be respected. This means (amongst other things) that we should remain mindful of children's cognitive vulnerability - of the fact that they are easily influenced and not very good at critically assessing views and arguments (by comparison with autonomous and well educated adults). Second, aiming to develop the pupil's capacity for autonomous rational judgement is a necessary element of education of any sort and part of what distinguishes education proper from such things as training, instruction and indoctrination. So, as educators, we should both respect children's lack of autonomy and attempt to make them more autonomous.

To develop this argument, we need to define more precisely the terms 'religious education', 'religious instruction' and 'religious indoctrination' which we introduced previously. We referred to religious education as 'teaching <u>about</u> religion'. We do not mean that religious education has to be simply a factual survey of the world's religions, a dreary catalogue of doctrines. Pupils will not properly come to understand religious beliefs unless they acquire some insight into <u>why</u> believers accept those beliefs, and that means that they need to be taught, among other things, the <u>reasons</u>

which believers put forward for their beliefs. However, if this is to count as genuine education, then it must be done with the intention of developing pupils' capacity to make their own rational judgements about the truth or falsity of religious beliefs. This development of the capacity for autonomous rational judgement in turn requires that pupils should be acquainted not only with the reasons which believers give in support of their beliefs, but also with the reasons which critics give for rejecting them, and with the reasons which are given in support of alternative belief systems.

By 'religious instruction' we mean the teaching of religious beliefs as true, and with the intention that pupils should come to accept them as true. There need not always be a conflict between 'education' and 'instruction' as we have defined them. In the case of a subject such as mathematics, for instance, they are likely to coincide. The best way of getting pupils to accept mathematical truths as true is to help them to understand the reasons why they are true. It is, however, difficult to see how religious education and religious instruction could be compatible, and this is because religious beliefs, unlike mathematical truths (at least at school level), are contested and controversial. A religious teacher might conscientiously teach all the reasons standardly offered for and against the various systems of religious belief, with the intention that pupils should be equipped to make their own judgements, and also with the sincere belief that pupils who make their own rational and autonomous judgements are likely to decide in favour of the teacher's own religion. The teacher who is committed to the activity of education cannot, however, simply teach that religion as true, since there are other rational judges who believe that the religion is false and can offer reasons in support of that view, and pupils who are to be genuinely educated must be acquainted with those reasons.

Our assertion that religious beliefs are contested beliefs is not just a descriptive claim. It is more than just the assertion that as a matter of fact some people reject religious beliefs. The fact that there are people who, for instance, deny that the Holocaust took place, does not mean that children should not be taught about the Holocaust. In the case of religious beliefs, the disagreements and disputes are deeper and more widespread, but our claim that religious beliefs are contested is also a normative claim - that people disagree on the matter <u>and that people can present good reasons on either side of the dispute,</u> reasons which are therefore inconclusive. It may be that there are religious believers who reject this claim - who think that their beliefs are not just true but obviously and incontestably true and that anyone who rejects them is not just mistaken but irrational. In that case they will think that religious education can properly take the form of instruction in the truths of religion, and our argument against them would have to start further back. Here we address ourselves to those who, even if they are committed believers, recognise that religious beliefs are beliefs about which people can with good reason disagree.

Given that religious beliefs are in this sense contested and controversial, we maintain that the teacher who provides religious instruction is likely to be engaged in the activity not of genuine education but of indoctrination. The term 'indoctrination' is an emotive one, and it is difficult to find a clear and agreed definition of it. We are taking 'religious indoctrination' to mean the teaching of religious beliefs <u>with the intention that they should be accepted regardless of the reasons for or against those beliefs and competing beliefs.</u> This definition captures effectively the most important standard connotations of the term. 'Indoctrination' in this sense is a stronger term than 'instruction', but religious instruction is in practice likely to be describable as 'indoctrination', since the religious teacher whose primary intention is that pupils should accept religious beliefs as true will have to ignore or play down the reasons which count against those beliefs. Indoctrination in the sense in which we're using the term does not necessarily involve manipulation or 'conditioning' or the use of threats and inducements. It need not involve an intent to deceive – the indoctrinator may well sincerely believe in the truth of the beliefs which are imparted. We will argue, nevertheless, that church schools are in practice likely to be committed to the activity of religious instruction and that, given the contested status of religious beliefs, this is likely to amount to a form of indoctrination rather than genuine education.

(4) Educators or Indoctrinators?

A good place to begin this section is the recent *Consultation Report* (December 2000) of the Church of England's Church Schools Review Group, chaired by Lord Dearing. Consider statements such as the following:

> Church schools are places where the faith is proclaimed and lived, and which therefore offer opportunities to pupils and their families to explore the truths of Christian faith, to develop spiritually and morally, and to have a basis for <u>choice</u> about Christian commitment. They are places where the beliefs and practices of other faiths will be respected.... Church schools are not, and should not be, agents of proselytism where pupils are <u>expected</u> to make a Christian commitment. (para.3.4)

That looks like an explicit disavowal of any attempt to indoctrinate pupils or to promote the non-autonomous acceptance of Christian beliefs. The Report identifies as one of the purposes of Church schools what it calls the 'service' purpose, which is 'to serve all humanity' and 'to offer education for its own sake' (3.10 and 1.3 - the full formulation is that 'the Church would wish to offer education for its own sake as a reflection of God's love for humanity', but let that pass). If the sole motivation of Church schools were indeed to offer education for its own sake, simply because education is a basic human need which ought to be met, then no one could object. They would be as acceptable and as admirable as, for example, the religious agencies such as Christian Aid and CAFOD which do an excellent job combating world poverty and promoting overseas aid and development. The report is however quite explicit that this should not be the sole purpose of Church schools. It recommends giving increased importance to what it calls the 'nurture' purpose (3.10), and this is summed up in the quotation from the former Archbishop of Canterbury, Robert Runcie, that 'engagement with children and young people in schools' will enable the Church to:

- Nourish those of the faith,
- Encourage those of other faiths,
- Challenge those who have no faith. (1.3)

Note the asymmetry in that formulation, to which we will return shortly.

The report recommends that, in order to further the 'nurture' purpose, Church schools should emphasise their <u>distinctiveness</u>. It makes much of the idea that Church schools have a distinctive 'ethos', and it offers the following as a minimum list of what this ethos should involve. Every Church school, it says, should:

- Ensure that the school is led by a head teacher who is committed, with the help of staff, to establish and maintain the Christian character of the school in its day to day activities and in the curriculum.
- Engage meaningfully in Christian worship every day.
- Offer a school life that incorporates the values of the Christian faith....
- Ensure that Religious Education is given at least 5% of school time and that the character and quality of religious education are a particular concern of the head teacher and the governing body.
- Observe the major Christian festivals and in schools in which other faiths are present ensure that those faiths are able to mark their major festivals with integrity.
- Maintain and develop an active and affirming relationship with a parish church.
- Proclaim that it is a Church of England school on its external signboard and on its stationery.
- In Voluntary Controlled schools strive as a long-term policy to have their quota of reserved teachers with a Christian background, especially in key posts within the school. (4.27)

Let us look more closely at this idea of the 'ethos' of religious schools, which is often said to make them popular with parents. This too admits of both a benign interpretation and a more troubling one. If it means that religious schools have a good record of promoting basic human values of consideration and respect for others, of honesty and fairness, and of embodying those values in the day to day life of the school, then that is to be welcomed. We do not know whether it is true that religious schools have a better track record than non-religious schools in this respect, and it is difficult to see how such a generalisation could be substantiated, but if it is true, then the proper response is for non-religious schools to learn from it and seek to emulate it. The report's list strongly indicates, however, that there is much more to the notion of the 'ethos' of a church school, which begins to look worryingly like a subtle and indirect form of indoctrination. For example, take the practice of insisting that pupils at a school engage in worship through prayer. You might think that requiring schoolchildren to say 'Amen' at the end of a Christian prayer is an inoffensive and harmless activity. However, as Blaise Pascal suggested in his *Pensées*, one of the most effective ways of developing a belief in the existence of God if you are not intellectually or emotionally inclined to have one is to act as if you already believe in God. Getting children to say 'Amen' in a public setting can be an indirect way of inducing such a belief, particularly when there is strong peer pressure to hold that belief. (Note incidentally that when non-religious pupils, including agnostics and atheists, are forced or strongly encouraged to utter public assent to religious assumptions, this is hardly calculated to promote the value of honesty. Rather than fostering ethical behaviour, such practices look more like training in deception.)

Consider another element in the proposed Christian 'ethos', that head teachers and a significant proportion of other teachers in such schools should be committed Christians. Whether they like it or not, teachers can be powerful role models and influences on pupils, and that influence is likely to be especially strong if the majority of teachers at a school have very similar religious beliefs. Many pupils form very strong relationships with their teachers, and as such can be extremely malleable. This is indeed part of the emotional experience of learning at school, and it can be a beneficial inspiration and motivation to learn, but it gives teachers a power about which they should be extremely wary. Part of a teacher's responsibility must be to help pupils develop the tools for their own thought and personal development. This is unlikely to be achieved when there are such strong forces for psychological dependence combined with a lack of variety of role models. In short, religious teachers in religious schools are able to exercise a powerful influence and should actively seek to limit that influence (in order to avoid non-autonomous belief acquisition amongst their pupils). It seems clear that the Church Schools Review Group *Consultation Report*, on the contrary, welcomes that influence as a way of promoting the Christian faith. Church schools, it is said:

> … will not actively seek to convert children from the faith of their parents, but pupils will experience what it is like to live in a community that celebrates the Christian faith; to work within a framework of discipline and yet to be confident of forgiveness; to begin to share the Christian's hope and the Christian experience ... (3.22)

Despite the disavowal of an intent to convert, the suggestion is that by living in a Christian community pupils will themselves come to share the Christian faith. Note the emphasis which the report places on recruiting Christian teachers and on helping them to move into senior positions (chapter 5), and on the role of the head teacher in creating 'a distinctive Christian community' by 'living the values that she or he seeks to establish and winning a willing acceptance of those values by staff in particular, but also by children and parents' (7.2). Since the values in question are said to be 'distinctively Christian', not just shared human values, the implication is that Christian teachers should seek to act as role models who will win pupils to the Christian faith.

Consider now the emphasis which Church of England schools, in common
with other religious schools, are encouraged to place on religious education:

* An important element in the distinctiveness of Church schools
* will lie in the emphasis on the quality of Religious Education,
* which whilst covering other faiths will give particular weight to
* the Christian faith as held by the Church of England. (para.4.33)

This runs counter to government guidelines on religious education, which
require state schools to educate their pupils about a variety of different
religious beliefs, but from which religious schools are exempt (we return to
this point below). Again it seems clear that the Church of England, like
other faiths, is happy to load the scales in its own favour in order to
promote its own beliefs. Recall the asymmetry of the report's statement of
its educational role, to:

* Nourish those of the faith,
* Encourage those of other faiths,
* Challenge those who have no faith.

As people of no faith we are happy to be challenged, and to have our
children challenged, but why should the Church and its schools be so
selective in their challenge? A genuine concern for the development of
pupils' autonomy would require that, as they mature and become
increasingly capable of rational reflection and argument, all pupils should
be challenged in their beliefs. When they are too young to do so, they
should be protected from the premature imposition of particular beliefs. As
they grow, they should be encouraged to examine their beliefs and to look
at them critically.

But must they not first have such beliefs, before they can come to
question them? Is there not something faintly absurd about the idea of
five-year-olds being encouraged to 'examine their beliefs', and if it can
be taken seriously, would this not be a recipe for producing shallow
sceptics who question everything and are committed to nothing? It is

true that there is more to education than learning to question things, and that children must first have a view of the world before they can be taught to examine it and question it. That, however, is something which they are in any case likely to have. They will come to school with beliefs and assumptions which they have acquired from their parents and in which they have thus far been brought up. Some will come with religious predispositions, others with secular ones. There is no reason why the view of the world which they have inherited from their family should not, even in primary school, be 'challenged' in the sense that they learn that there are other views which other children equally take for granted. It is not the proper task of the school to give them these views. It is the task of education to enable them, gradually and in due course, to assess such views for themselves and to decide which of them to adopt as their own.

Is this the educational goal which the Church of England, and other religious groups, are prepared to espouse, or do they simply want to promote their own beliefs? We think that they, and all concerned, should be frank about this. If they genuinely wish to promote education for its own sake, we can have no objection. Our clear impression, however, is that they want more religious schools because they wish to enjoy a privileged position in forming the beliefs of the pupils of such schools. In that case they can have no business in asking for state support for such schools. As a matter of fact, any religious schools which seek to mould the beliefs of their pupils, even if they do not obtain financial support from the state, are to be deprecated. This is because, in so doing, they both impede the development of children's autonomy and encourage children non-autonomously to acquire religious (and other significant) beliefs. We are not arguing for the banning of independent religious schools on those grounds; there are obvious wider political objections to any such ban, which would give the state far too much power in relation to other social institutions. We do argue that religious schools which have a partisan purpose, and which seek unduly to influence their pupils' beliefs, thereby forfeit any claim to state support.

Our objector may still insist that we exaggerate the power of religious schools. 'Give us a child for the first seven years', the Jesuits claimed, 'and he is ours for life', but we know that they were wrong. The familiar adage 'Once a Catholic, always a Catholic' is not literally true. People do break away from the religious beliefs in which they were raised. They are not for ever imprisoned in the orthodoxy which they were once taught. Indeed, it may be said that it is healthy for children first to be taught uncritically a firm set of beliefs, which in due course they can then examine for themselves, if only to give them something against which to rebel. To say this, however, is to underestimate the extent to which beliefs and attitudes acquired in people's formative years may be hard to escape even after they have been consciously rejected. Many adults brought up within strict religions are psychologically burdened with guilt and self-loathing long after they have jettisoned the religious beliefs which give rise to these. It is also to underestimate the real anguish which many people feel when they find themselves doubting the faith in which they were raised. They often have to struggle against internalised guilt and social pressure in order to decide what they really believe. It should not be the task of educational institutions to make it more difficult for people to make up their own minds about the truth or falsity of religious beliefs.

We have argued that religious schools, even if they do not crudely proselytise or indoctrinate, tend to inhibit the growth of their pupils' autonomy by giving them a one-sided view of the world and by exercising various kinds of pressure. They also often fail to meet the requirements of full information and voluntariness and so their promotion of religious beliefs can justifiably be characterised as a form of indoctrination.

In the light of this, we return to our earlier three arguments, which can now be refined. Recall first the point about evidence. It is too simple to argue against religious schools on the grounds that schools should teach only evidence-based beliefs, and that religious beliefs do not come into that category. There is however a subtler point to be made about the relation between beliefs and the evidence for them. It is part of the job of education to teach pupils to recognise the differing status of different kinds of beliefs and of different kinds of evidence. Religious beliefs are different in kind from scientific or mathematical ones and pupils need to learn this. They have not properly understood the nature of religious beliefs if they have not been encouraged to recognise that such beliefs are controversial and are contested. There may be evidence for such beliefs, but rational judges may reach conflicting conclusions about their truth or falsity. We alluded earlier to the disputed status of literary judgements. Are these evidence-based beliefs? If they are, then the way in which they can be supported by evidence is different from the way in which, for instance, scientific hypotheses can be supported by evidence, and that in turn is different from the relation between historical claims and the evidence for them. It is an important part of education that pupils should come to understand these differing ways in which statements can be supported by evidence. No academic discipline should be taught uncritically, but a scientific education involves coming to recognise how scientific hypotheses can be tested, how as a result of repeated testing they may come to be well established, and how the rejection of a scientific belief has to meet those standards of evidence. In contrast, a literary education involves learning that the relation between critical judgements and the evidence for them is much more a matter for personal assessment. A pupil who simply learns 'the right answers' to critical questions about literary texts has not understood what literary education is all about. Religious beliefs are different again. There is a long tradition of rational debate and argument about them, of attempted proofs and refutations, which appeal to publicly shared standards of rationality and aspire to a kind of objectivity. In that respect they are different from literary judgements, but on the other hand they have not achieved the kind of consensus which supports well-established scientific theories. A genuine religious education will teach this. Pupils are misled if they are not taught that questions such as whether there are gods, or whether human beings can survive physical death, are open questions. Religious schools, in view of their self-proclaimed purpose, are, to say the least, not well placed to do this.

This takes us back also to the 'neutrality' argument. We argued that state schools should be neutral with respect to religious beliefs. We noted that there are other ways in which a certain kind of neutrality can be achieved. If the neutrality that is wanted is an even-handedness between different sections of the population, then that could as well be attained by state-funding for a variety of different kinds of religious school, instead of state-funding which favours some religions rather than others. We still have to examine the practical objections to such an approach, but in the meantime we note that it would not meet the case for neutrality which is more closely linked to the autonomy argument. That case is that education should take a neutral position on questions which are deeply contested open questions. The truth or falsity of religious belief is such a question, on which pupils should therefore be helped to make their own rational judgements, not pressured into the acceptance of one particular answer.

Should education then be neutral on every matter on which people disagree? Should it treat every question as an open question? No. We do not think, for instance, that scientific education should be neutral as between the theory of evolution and creationism. There are of course people who accept creationism, but their defence of it simply does not meet the same standards of evidence which scientific theories can meet. We realise that that argument potentially gives rise to an infinite regress - but not all potentially infinite regresses are vicious regresses. If someone claims that creationism <u>does</u> meet scientific standards of evidence, we can move the argument up to that level. For the purpose of that argument, it will probably be possible to agree on what count as standards of good scientific evidence – and by those standards the creationists are simply wrong, even if they cannot be brought to accept the fact. Disagreements about the truth or falsity of religious belief are not like that. Rational disputants can agree to differ on the matter, while recognising one another as rational, and it is for that reason that religious education should proceed on the basis of neutrality.

What about basic human values? Should rejection of racism or sexism, for instance, be treated as open questions just because some people are racist or sexist? Up to a point, yes. Even basic values of respect and concern for others should not be imposed in authoritarian fashion. Pupils should be encouraged to think about them and argue about them in an open-minded way. We accept, however, that in this case too there are limits to neutrality. Schools as institutions should not and cannot be neutral with respect to basic human values. They should embody in their activities the values of mutual concern and respect, of honesty and fairness, and they should seek to impart those values to their pupils. Such values are the foundations of any minimally decent community, and it is right that they should be built into the activities of all schools. Religious beliefs are not part of this minimal consensus. They are located on a terrain which is more deeply contested, it is appropriate that schools should recognise this fact, and that does require neutrality on their part.

As we have previously indicated, we think that this is an argument which religious believers themselves can accept. The committed Christian or Hindu or Muslim will, we suppose, regard their religious commitment as more than just that of any minimally decent human being. They will see it as a real choice, one which sets them apart from others, and is a distinctive and authentic expression of their identity. A deep commitment of that kind is not something which can be entered into simply because of a lack of awareness of alternatives, or in response to the pressure to conform. Religious schools are inherently liable to foster religious beliefs which are, in that sense, inauthentic.

We return finally to our first, crudely stated, argument:

- Religious belief is undesirable.
- Religious schools encourage religious belief.
- Whatever encourages something undesirable is itself undesirable.
- Therefore: Religious schools are undesirable.

As it stands, the first premise is extremely simplistic. Such a crude generalisation cannot, for instance, be sustained in the face of the wealth of examples of cultural and artistic achievements, of humane reforms and struggles for justice, which have been religiously inspired. Nevertheless there is a certain distinctive form which religious belief can take, and when it does so it is indeed 'undesirable. Our case against religious schools has assumed that religious beliefs should be autonomously selected, on the basis of evidence and rational judgement, and with a willingness to recognise and respond to criticisms. Many religious believers would share this assumption, but some would not. There are religious believers of a fundamentalist kind, for whom religion is a matter of unquestioned faith and dogma, to be maintained despite the evidence rather than because of it. We do not suggest that the advocates of religious schools consciously intend to foster this kind of religious belief. We do suggest that, inadvertently at least, they risk fostering it. And that is part of the case against religious schools.

(5) In Defence of Religious Schools?

So much for the basic case against religious schools. Let us now turn to the case which might be mounted in defence of such schools, and in defence of state support for them. We will consider in turn claims about the quality of education provided by religious schools, claims which invoke parents' rights, and claims about the desirability of supporting a range of religious schools to reflect the multi-cultural character of contemporary England.

(a) Quality of Education

It is often claimed that religious schools (on average) provide a better education than their secular counterparts. Ofsted, for instance, recently declared that Anglican schools 'are not only academically successful but also boast a good 'ethos' and well behaved pupils' (*Independent on Sunday*, 27/8/00). This claim, in turn, is often used as an argument in favour of religious schools. There are, however, several objections to this line of argument.

First, there are good reasons for doubting whether religious schools are quite as successful as is sometimes suggested. For one thing, it is quite possible that religious parents have, for whatever reason, better behaved or more academic children. These children, then, would flourish in almost any school. More to the point perhaps, while most Church schools are not officially permitted to select children on their basis of their class, behaviour or intelligence, there is little doubt that selection does take place. Sometimes this is inadvertent. Precisely because they have a good reputation, religious schools are sought out by ambitious and resourceful parents, both believers and non-believers; and as these tend to be the sort of parents who produce ambitious and resourceful children, high standards are perpetuated. But selection frequently takes a more active form. Church schools often have more applicants than ordinary community schools, and they also tend to have more control in selecting one applicant over another, so they are frequently in a position to select well behaved and able children, once again perpetuating their high standing. Indeed, many people who support the principles of comprehensive education are opposed to Church schools not, or not only, because of their confessional character, but because many of them operate as 'grammar schools by another name'. Finally, there is some evidence that religious schools are concentrated in better-off areas. For all these reasons, and while acknowledging the remarkable achievement of some religious schools in providing outstanding schooling, we should treat the proposition that 'religious schools are generally better than non-religious ones' with some caution. Furthermore, given the ambiguity of the evidence for the success of religious schools, better comparative data on religious and community schools (admissions policies, teaching methods and curricula, the attitudes and values of their pupils etc) should be collected before making major decisions about provision.[2]

---

[2] The better performance of church schools has been related to lower levels of deprivation amongst their pupils, for example: "Analysis of levels of examination performance in comparison with levels of free school meal entitlement shows that once the different levels of free school meal entitlement are taken into account, the differences in GCSE/GNVQ examination performance and absenteeism [between church and other schools] were not statistically significant." (*Church School Secondary Education in Wales, Examination and Attendance Data, 2000*, National Assembly for Wales)

But even if we grant, for the sake of argument, that religious schools do, as things stand, offer their pupils a better education than non-religious ones, there are still grounds for rejecting the suggestion that this is good reason to favour them. Instead one might argue that community schools should learn from religious schools and adopt whatever it is in their practice – strict discipline, active involvement of parents, close ties with the local community - that accounts for their success. It is hardly right, after all, to expect parents who send their children to ordinary community schools to accept second best.

(b) The Rights of Parents

It is often suggested that by supporting religious schools, the government is offering parents more <u>choice</u>. Our case against religious schools has itself been rooted in a concern about choice: that such schools undermine the development of pupils' capacity to make their own independent choices about fundamental beliefs. Can this concern be trumped by an appeal to parental choice? Should we attach some special importance to parents' choice of the kind of education they want for their children? Perhaps what is being invoked is some general principle about <u>parents' rights</u>. The *Human Rights Act* (1998) suggests that we should take seriously 'the right of parents to ensure such education and teaching in conformity with their own religious and philosophical convictions'. But what exactly does such a right amount to, and does it entail the recognition of a right of parents to have their children educated in religious schools?

An obvious first answer is that parents have rights to bring up their own children as they see best. Parents make choices for their children about the kind of life they can and should lead – about what books they read, what games they play, what television programmes they watch, what food they eat. Why should parents not be allowed to determine what religious beliefs and practices their children follow? Moreover, the exercise of a religion is extremely important to those people who have one; it can be, and often is, a central part of their lives. Religious parents obviously want to pass on to their own offspring values, doctrines, and practices that they regard as of the first importance.

There is surely also a huge difference between teaching a child <u>about</u> a religion and passing on that same religion to the child. Some religious parents will be unhappy with an education that merely provides children with information, however full and sympathetic, about their religion, but which treats it as one amongst many possible faiths. For the parent for whom religion is the supreme and absolute truth, an invaluable and irreplaceable guide to the meaning of her life, and a condition of her own salvation, it should be nothing less for her children. Her children should thus, she may argue, be taught by those for whom this religion is <u>their</u> life.

Parents do have rights to bring up children. But it should not be thought that parents have these rights in virtue of somehow owning their own children. Children are not the property of their parents or indeed of anybody, although it is unfortunately true that we continue to speak as if this, or something very like it, is true. It is equally misguided to see the lives of children as somehow only an extension of their parents' lives. Children are separate if not yet fully independent people. Children may not have the same moral and political status as adults. But they do have their own interests that should be protected. The crucial question is not whether it is best for the parents that their children be given a religious schooling but whether it is best for the children themselves that they are. Most parents do act in the best interests of their children but the simple fact of being a parent does not mean that their choices for their children are automatically the best.

Moreover, it is one thing for parents in private to bring up their children to believe what they, the parents, think true and important. It is quite another for parents to expect that the state should undertake the role of transmitting such a belief. The state has its own interest in ensuring that children grow up to be responsible and capable citizens. It must design a system of education that serves that end, as well as promoting the interests of children.

But should not the state respect the right of everyone to practise their chosen religion? And is not giving to one's children a religious schooling an essential part of what it is for the members of a family to practise their religion? Again, it is consistent with the right of adults to live according to their own faith that their children should participate in the practices, rituals, ceremonies, and activities of that faith. This is true so long as the practice of the religion does not violate the rights of non-believers, and so long as the children's participation in this practice is neither coerced nor harmful to their own interests.

But even if this is the case, the right of parents to practise their religion does not impose on the state an obligation to provide their children with a religious school of the parents' choice. At most it requires the state not to prevent families from practising their religion. That could involve private instruction of children in the religion's tenets and their involvement in regular religious activities. It cannot mean state-funded or state-assisted single-religion schools.

But can a religious parent be content with a publicly funded education which does not confirm and reinforce the truth of what is being transmitted to the child in private? Is it not deeply damaging to a child to learn one thing from her parents and quite another from her school? And is it not offensive to religious believers to have their deeply held beliefs publicly questioned by teachers? These complaints would be warranted if religious education sought to teach that religious belief – in general or in some particular case – was disreputable. But a religious education which teaches that those beliefs which a child is led to endorse at home constitute but one amongst many religions does not of itself show disrespect for these beliefs. It is perfectly possible to represent these beliefs accurately and dispassionately without either endorsing or repudiating them.

(c) The Rights of Communities

We turn now to a related but different case which might be made, appealing not to the rights of individuals (such as those of particular parents) but rather to <u>collective</u> rights, the <u>rights of communities</u>. Collective subscription to a particular religion is one of the ways, often one of the most important ways, in which the identity of a community is expressed, affirmed and celebrated. Consider the relationship between Judaism and the Jewish community, or consider how their religions help maintain the identity of some of the Asian communities in Britain. When religion is considered within this context, is it not clear that religious schools and religious instruction are means by which a community can preserve its identity? By passing its constitutive beliefs on to the next generation a community is able to reproduce itself over time. If the community is denied the possibility of educating its own young in its religious beliefs then it may be in danger of losing its identity and of disappearing. Does not the ideal of cultural pluralism demand a collective right to religious schools?

Considered in the abstract, the argument looks as unconvincing as the appeal to parents' rights. Again, it appears to consider children as the property of adults and as instruments to be used for the latter's ends. If a group wishes to survive it is wrong that it should treat its own children as the means whereby a guaranteed future is assured. It does this when it so educates its children that they have no real choice but to be the bearers of the group's identity. Recall what was said earlier about the vital importance of the development and exercise of autonomy for the life of the individual. It follows from this that children should be allowed and encouraged to decide for themselves, autonomously, about their basic beliefs and life-stance. This principle is breached when children are instructed into adherence to a particular religion for the sake of maintaining and affirming the identity of the religious group. Children should not be treated as merely the means to a group's ends.

Before rejecting this argument, however, we should look at it in a more specific historical context, that of contemporary England as a multi-cultural society. Recall the facts about the present existence and character of state-supported religious schools. They are overwhelmingly Christian, and these schools make up a substantial minority of schools in the state sector. This gives Christian religious groups, in particular the Church of England and the Roman Catholic Church, a power and a presence out of all proportion to the size of their committed membership. In a multi-cultural England, should not other religious groups such as Muslims and Sikhs also have their own state-supported religious schools, and should we not welcome the fact that in the last few years this has begun to happen?

There is a simple argument from fairness and consistency here. There are also deeper arguments about the nature of multi-culturalism and pluralism. The recent report of the Commission established by the Runnymede Trust, the 'Parekh Report' on *The Future of Multi-Ethnic Britain,* has some pertinent things to say about this, which we should take seriously. It points to what it sees as the limitations of a traditional liberal interpretation of equality and tolerance. Liberalism affirms the equality of individual citizens in the public sphere. This entails that the public political culture should be neutral as between different cultural traditions and values, and that the particular cultural (including religious) allegiances of individuals are to be confined to the private sphere.

That is not, of course, the situation we find in contemporary England. The public political culture is not neutral with respect to different cultural traditions. There is an established church, and it occupies a privileged position in the life of society generally and the education system in particular. The appropriate response might be to call for disestablishment and to argue for a more consistent liberalism, but it may also be that the realities of political life point to the limitations of liberalism as a political philosophy. Its weakness is the sharp division it makes between the public and the private spheres. The public sphere cannot, it may be argued, be neutral as between different cultural traditions and values. The alternatives then are either that the public political sphere reflects a single dominant culture to the exclusion of others, or that it reflects the diversity of cultures. The liberal model of equality may need to be challenged by a pluralist model, which *The Future of Multi-Ethnic Britain* defines thus:

> ...it rejects the hard and fast distinction between public and private realms, and envisages that the public realm should be continually revised to accommodate cultural diversity in society at large. Unlike the liberal view, this model does not place the political culture beyond negotiation, and it maintains that recognition, as distinct from toleration, should be a central value. (p.43)

Underpinning this 'politics of recognition' is the idea that cultural and religious allegiances are identity-conferring, and that equal citizenship requires that these identity-conferring allegiances are not just tolerated but publicly recognised. So, to return to the case of religious schools, the fact that there is state support for 4716 Church of England schools, 2108 Roman Catholic schools, but only 30 Jewish schools and 1 Sikh school[3], is not just an inconsistency, but a public statement about the status of different cultural identities. Some are recognised, some are virtually invisible, and that invisibility is felt by the individuals who belong to these cultural groups and who are forced to see themselves as marginalised second-class citizens.

The argument from consistency is a powerful one. If there is to be continuing state support for Christian schools, then there is a case for providing the same support for Muslim schools, Sikh schools, and others. Having said that, however, we should also acknowledge the clear limits to the argument.

---

[3] DfEE statistics on Schools in England 2000, since when at least 1 Muslim school has gained public funding.

First, it is emphatically not an argument for the expansion of state support for Church of England or Roman Catholic schools. On the contrary, greater even-handedness could as well be achieved by a drastic curtailing of support for Christian schools as by increasing support for non-Christian religious schools.

Secondly, it is to be doubted whether separate schools for every religious persuasion are really the best way of promoting pluralism and tolerance in a multi-cultural society. Providing a full range of sectarian schools in every district would in any case be impracticable, except perhaps in the very largest cities. More importantly, if children grow up within a circumscribed culture, if their friends and peers are mostly from the same religion and hence also, very likely, the same ethnic group, and if they rarely meet or learn to live with others from different backgrounds, this is hardly calculated to promote the acceptance and recognition of diversity. We have clear evidence to the contrary from Northern Ireland, where the separation of Catholic schools and Protestant schools has played a significant part in perpetuating the sectarian divide.

Thirdly, having acknowledged the importance of recognising diverse cultural identities, we still have to balance that against the importance of individual autonomy. Agreed, our identity is not just constituted by the choices we make as autonomous individuals, but, equally, it is constituted by more than just the cultural, religious or ethnic groups to which we belong. How to balance individual autonomy against cultural identity is a question perhaps impossible to answer in the abstract, but we can give it a specific answer in the context of education. The family is the primary institution through which cultural identities are conferred and transmitted. In early childhood especially we begin by identifying ourselves with the groups to which our parents belong.

In contrast to the role of the family, it is the role of the school above all to make the growing child aware of wider perspectives, of other ways of seeing the world, other cultural groups and traditions. It is the job of education to equip the child with the ability to stand back from his or her inherited beliefs and assumptions, and with the capacity to make his or her own rational critical judgements and choices. We return therefore to the autonomy argument as the heart of the case against religious schools.

(6) Conclusions and Policy Recommendations

Our arguments support three key principles which we believe must guide policy-making with regards to religious schools:

1. <u>In a free and open society, beliefs about fundamental religious and value commitments should be adopted autonomously and voluntarily.</u> Attempts to indoctrinate either children or adults, by taking advantage of their lack of competence, or by withholding or misrepresenting relevant information and arguments, or by using of coercion or manipulation, breach this principle. This autonomy principle has been at the heart of many of our arguments. It is one which most people, including many religious believers, do in fact endorse – and one which all reasonable people should endorse.

2. <u>Neither parents nor faith communities have a right to call upon the state to help them inculcate their particular religious beliefs in their children, nor further their own projects, customs or values through their children.</u> Children are not the property of their parents or faith communities, nor merely an extension of their parents' lives. This means that 'parental choice' and 'community rights' are not trump cards which can be used to justify any choice made for children.

3. <u>In a pluralist, multi-cultural society, the state must promote the tolerance and recognition of different values, religious beliefs and non-religious beliefs.</u> The state should not pursue any policy which is likely to lead to decreased toleration or recognition of the rights of others to hold different beliefs and values from our own.

If we were designing the education system from scratch, the logical consequence of these principles would be that there would be no religious schools at all. Although the second two principles cover only the state's role in religious schooling, the first, and arguably most important, principle conflicts with any attempt to bring up children with knowledge of only one religious tradition. Children educated in many religious schools lack the information to make an independent decision as to whether they wish to adopt that religion's beliefs, and the 'ethos' of a religious school is potentially coercive or otherwise inappropriately influential. Therefore, any religious school, including independent ones, may contravene the principle.

Even without this first principle, the second and third count against the state's actively supporting religious schools. The second holds that parents have no right to expect the state to help them instruct or induct their children into their religion, and so removes any obligation on the state to support religious schools. The third gives the state a positive reason to refuse to help religious schools, since encouraging children to be educated wholly within a particular religion, where what is usually taught is that the religion in question is 'the one truth', does not help promote a society where recognition of the legitimacy of others' beliefs and values is recognised.

However, it would be wishful thinking, from a humanist point of view, to believe that the abolition of all religious schools, or at least the withdrawal of state funds from them, is a practical proposal. Such a move would certainly meet with a lot of resistance. It would also be extremely disruptive, at a time where there are enough challenges for our education system already. Despite the widespread belief that philosophers deal with utopias and not the real world, we do not wish to make any proposal that stands no chance of being implemented. Therefore, although abolition of, or withdrawal of funding for, religious schools is a course of action we advocate, we do not expect to see such a radical reform implemented. Instead, we would make three practical recommendations that would help close the gap between our three principles and the status quo.

1. The state should not support the further expansion of religious schools. Given that the very existence of any state-funded religious school contradicts the principles which we have argued should govern state policy towards religious education, any move to increase their number is unacceptable. This would, unfortunately, leave us with an unequal situation – one in which the Christian religions have thousands of schools, while other religions have a mere handful. However, increasing the number of non-Christian religious schools is a poor way of dealing with this injustice. In general, we do not believe that two wrongs make a right, or that the best way to deal with a situation where one group has, for historical reasons, been permitted to do something against the best interests of society is to extend this permission to other groups. We consider that a better way of addressing the injustice is by means of our second recommendation.

2. The application of government guidelines requiring 'multi-faith' religious education should be extended to cover religious schools. At present, state schools must, by law, cover a variety of different religious beliefs as part of the religious studies curriculum. Religious schools, however, are exempted from this compulsion. This is incompatible with the principles we have argued for here. It undermines recognition and tolerance of others' beliefs by not giving them equal status on the syllabus. It stifles the development of children's autonomy, by denying them information about alternative beliefs. And it makes use of the resources of the state to help impose the religious beliefs of parents onto their children. If religious schools are to be allowed to continue, they must all therefore make a sincere attempt to include in their religious education an objective, fair and balanced treatment of other belief systems.

3. The legal requirements for and guidelines on 'multi-faith' religious education should be modified to include the compulsory teaching of non-religious views, such as atheism and Humanism. Reform of the system of religious education is incomplete unless it properly recognises the importance of non-religious views. Children are not given the full picture unless they are aware that there are secular alternatives to religious belief. Nor is a society genuinely pluralistic if it recognises the importance and legitimacy of religions, but not that of non-religious viewpoints. However, at the moment, the guidelines governing religious education in state schools do not explicitly require the inclusion of atheism, agnosticism, or Humanism on the syllabus. This is despite the fact that at least a quarter of the population is atheist or agnostic. Unless this is rectified, any work done to promote an inclusive society by encouraging recognition and understanding of beliefs different from our own is severely undermined.

These recommendations and the arguments for them are made from an unashamedly humanist viewpoint. However, as humanist philosophers, we believe that issues such as these must be resolved, not by an appeal to dogma or creed, but by appeal to principles and arguments that rational people should accept. We believe the arguments of this pamphlet are in the spirit of this commitment. The religious and the non-religious have an equal concern that beliefs are adopted autonomously, that children are not just the pawns of their parents or communities, and that we build an inclusive, multi-cultural society. Our arguments are therefore not sticks with which to beat the religious, but appeals to reason which we believe the religious too should embrace. All of us, religious, agnostic or atheist, have reason to ensure that religious schools do not increase in number, and are reformed to be compatible with a decent, tolerant society.